# The DIARY of

# OREO VAN TYKE

**BY *EILEEN TIDWELL***

## 1996

Kelly Van Twist foals a horse colt. The amount of white on this foal make him easy to notice. The sire of the foal is American Paint Horse Champion Van Tyke, who is also the sire of Kelly.

*Oreo Van Tyke as a baby in 1996*

Erna Ginkel, the owner of these horses, is casting a critical eye at this startlingly white foal, expressing disappointment that he does not have more color (spots). But she is happy that the spots he does have will be black. At this point they look grayish.

I have gone over to see the new addition and I keep telling her, "Hey, I LOVE the way he is colored; he's so different."(Black and white paints have never been my favorites... I like the bay paints. But this little guy really grabbed my attention.) "Plus," I say, "This is as good a foal as I have ever seen. Truly."

This foal had a hip and shoulder that were unreal. Plus a cute head; well, he was just doggone good all over! Now, I am a Quarter Horse breeder. I have had a paint or two, but not in a long time. At home I have some outstanding Quarter Horse colts of my own.

I add, "I hope you hurry up and sell him because he is going to be worth too much money and I can't afford him!" (This is a very good foal, a very well-bred foal, and at the height of the black and white boom, he has the right colors. Sure he is worth more than I can afford!!) Besides, I don't need another breed of horse and I don't need a stallion right now.. . . I'm trying to convince myself to just forget this colt!

As a weanling, he has been with a trainer for a short time and has been successfully shown at halter.

Shortly after that his owner has sold him for a pretty decent sum (more than I could have scraped up!), to a veterinarian who already owns two Van Tyke stallions. My pocketbook sighs with relief; my heart sort of sags.

# 1997

In the spring of 1997 I see Oreo again. (Erna named him Oreo because, naturally, of his black and white color...plus, I suspect, she thinks the big marking on one hip and flank, looks a bit like a large Oreo cookie that is missing a couple of bites.)

He is still a smashing looking colt and is still playful and friendly and seems exceptionally bright. I congratulate the veterinarian on this colt that I am so enamored of.

In December of 1997 I am told that Oreo is for sale!

My guess is that three stallions, all brothers, are beginning to be a bit much for this busy veterinarian.

I inquire what the bottom dollar is. I gulp when I'm told. The price is a bargain, actually, it is just that it is beyond my means, especially since I am unemployed!

But I keep thinking about it. Can't get that colt out of my mind. I call and make an offer. Eventually we come to a price that I can manage...*IF* I can get three of my other horses sold. And raise some money to go with that...IF IF.......

## 1998

*Oreo being started under saddle, 1998*

I've sold my good reining horse; I've sold my antique Cadillac. I have the money.

So in January 1998 Oreo becomes my horse and immediately goes to my friend and trainer Rick Smith, who excels in starting colts. I have sold three horses, including my reining horse, plus I have sold my vintage 1964 Cadillac. Now I am broke, but Oreo is mine and I'm not in debt for him.

The grapevine hears that I have this good black and white paint stallion. People begin coming by to see him, and/or calling to see if I am booking mares.

Booking Mares?!!! He wasn't even two yet! Mercy.

No, I am saying, I am not booking mares. I am not standing him to the public. This paint colt is for me to enjoy. Hopefully he will prove to be a good sire eventually, but probably never stand to the public. Too much hassle. Too much trouble. No. I'm going to train and ride and enjoy this horse and hopefully even show him a little. I do love to train an intelligent, athletic young horse.

I leave Oreo with Rick for 60 days; I want this colt completely gentle and used to the unexpected. I am sixty years old and I don't break youngsters any more. I just want to do their serious training.

I watch him being ridden and love his gorgeous action. He moves as nicely as any horse I have ever owned.

By mid March, I have gone out to Rick's and caught the colt up, saddled and ridden him alone. I feel comfortable with him.

*Riding Oreo in my training pen 1998*

I bring the colt home April 1st, going nicely in a snaffle bit, quiet for the most part and still the fun-loving character he has always been. He is gentle and well started, with very little buck.

Now we begin his serious training.

June through August

During the summer I have ridden Oreo probably an average of twice a week. I have gone slow with his training because I constantly remind myself that this is only a two year old colt, regardless of how far along he is and how mature he looks.

His fun and games emphasize the colt thing, for sure. This is a hilarious horse.

I see him playing with all kinds of makeshift toys. One of his favorite playthings is an orange traffic cone he found on the place. He loves to grab it in his teeth and run, waving it over his head.

He thoroughly enjoys ropes too and will take a rope in his teeth and nod his head until he gets the rope to spinning wildly. This goes on and on.

One day I spotted him chasing one of our steers, waving a tree limb as they raced around the trap they were sharing.

*Oreo playing with buggy whip*

Several times I have spied him doing these things as I sit at the computer in my studio but by the time I grab the video camera, check the tape and run outside, he has gone on to something else. He needs to be on film or tape. He has to be one of America's funniest pets.

Oreo's Advance Training Begins - He has had a nice start with Rick, but he doesn't back well at all. Part of what I do during the summer is work on his backing.

*Relaxing in the back yard*

My method is to use a gag bit, a snaffle that is on a bridle that pulls through the bit, putting pressure on the mouth corners and also behind the ears. This is a very, very mild bit, but can exert considerable leverage. To teach a horse to back, I hold both reins steady with enough contact to prevent the horse from moving forward and I ask for the backup with leg pressure....he knows to move from pressure, but he can't go forward so logically he will back. However, Oreo balks and leans back only grudgingly moving a leg when he has to.

So in his case, I see-saw the bit....I keep steady pressure on both reins, but then I put slightly more pressure on one side, squeezing with legs and saying "back." He has to take a step back on the side that is getting the extra pressure. I immediately release the extra pressure on that side. Then, still maintaining fairly light pressure on BOTH reins, I apply extra pressure to the other side. When he moves one or both legs on that side, I release.

At first I am only asking for one or two steps on each side, then I release all pressure and place my hand on his neck and let him stand quietly.

In a few sessions, he has quit bowing his neck and leaning into his haunches and is backing willingly and quietly.

Along with those lessons, I have been working on getting a 180 degree turn around on the rear end. I "lead" with the inside rein and apply some pressure low toward the shoulder with the outside rein...His nose is being led into the turn, but the pressure on the corner of the mouth on the outside is pushing his shoulder over as well. My outside leg bumps him to keep the whole body following into the turn.

He is coming along quite well.

## Starting on Cattle

*Starting to follow cattle, hot summer-time riding wear for me!*

I give him two short sessions on tracking calves, a start for cutting or working cow horse. I put my two calves in the pen and just follow them around the first time...a total of maybe 5 or 6 minutes.

The next time I start "heading" them on the fence....following along with them, and then taking a short cut to pass by them and turn to face them, making them turn back up the fence.

At the end of these two sessions, he is actually trying to anticipate their moves himself.

I unsaddle him thinking to myself, this could be a $50,000 cutting horse if he just had the opportunity!

## September 1998

I have had Oreo turned out with Poky, our little 17 year old unregistered quarter mare. I want him to learn to have manners with mares, and Poky has done a nice job of doing that. When she comes in heat, he very clumsily starts learning to be a stallion. However, I don't witness an actual breeding. She's pretty short tempered and impatient with him. She's teaching him quickly that he must pay attention to the ladies' moods. He is getting some basic lessons in manners.

Somehow though while they have been turned out together, he has managed to get a pretty deep cut on a front foot, low on the pastern, but not into the hoof. It requires bandages and medications all throughout September.

## October 22, 1998

Oreo continues to entertain and flabbergast me with the things he dreams up to do.

Today during our pre-ride warm-up, I had run the bridle reins across the saddle and secured each one to the saddle rear cinch.

The bridle is a gag with snaffle and is rigged as German martingale. With the reins secured this way, he can still flex and have plenty of head room, but not get his head all the way down to buck.

Usually.

I turned Oreo loose in the training pen and took my buggy (lunging) whip to signal him to exercise, the routine I use when I think he may be too full of himself and ready to buck a little.

He wasn't too interested in running around the pen and bucking like he usually does. Instead he decided he would prefer to roll.

I managed to get him up before he could do more than lie down, but somehow, and I have no idea how, he managed to slip the entire bridle off his head. I dropped the whip and walked toward him to catch him before he could damage my dragging bridle.

But he took off, not real fast, but obviously wanting to play some games...my bridle was dragging between his front feet and I was cringing with every step he took, because that rig cost in the neighborhood of $50. Being among the retired/unemployed, I don't need to spend another wad on replacing this bridle.

Well, this little boy spies my buggy whip lying on the ground and makes a beeline for it. He grabs it up in his mouth and goes trotting and cantering about the pen waving the whip in the air.

Naturally I have no camera on me.

Eventually I catch him and get the bridle back on him and lead him up to my "mounting block", a big tractor tire in the center of the pen.

He's getting too tall for me to struggle up on now, with my short, fat, arthritic legs, so he has learned to move up parallel to whatever I am using as a mounting block.

After a fairly short arena workout, I took him out into a larger area and did some various drills with him: slow 360s, backing up hill, etc.

Then a new lesson: I opened the gates to the outside and rode him out onto the street, back and forth around the street right of way by our house, and then a little way down the street and around an orchard area.

Coming back up the street a neighbor called out and I stopped to visit for awhile, which was good for the horse. For the most part, he stood quietly.

Then we continued toward the house, and stopped again to visit with another neighbor for awhile.

All in all, a pretty good little workout and rather entertaining, too, what with his buggy whip shenanigans.

In early November his breeder, Erna Ginkel, comes over and rides him for the first time. Who better to appreciate him than the lady responsible for his being here!

*Oreo and Erna Ginkel*

## November 1998

My biggest challenge with this playful young stallion is disciplining him about his biting. He does not bite at me in a mean way, but he is obsessed with grabbing things, including my clothes and possibly even my flesh, in his mouth.

No one knows better than I do that this could be extremely dangerous, so I'm experimenting with different methods of discipline. Pushing him away only made him act like he thought I was playing, too.

Slapping - ditto.

This week I took a rather large stick to him, whacking him hard; that seems to have helped. This is apparently going to be a challenge.

LATE NOVEMBER: Oreo is unusually quiet one day as I ride. I return to the barn and take his temperature. He feels hot to touch.

Thermometer reads 106 degrees!

Naturally I rush in and call the vet. Then I begin hosing his legs with cool water and wet bath towels and hang them over his head and neck. By the time the vet comes his temperature is down considerably, but we dose him with meds for the fever and antibiotics for whatever must be going on. He never really shows any outward signs of illness, does cough some. I kept him on antibiotics for four days and then stayed off him for another week. No problems. No after-effects, either.

When I checked my mares at our distant pasture, I found them exhibiting similar symptoms minus fever, within the month. Seems to be a respiratory thing going around, something that the vaccines don't cover.

## January 10, 1999

I took Oreo for a trailer ride yesterday down to the cutting trainer who originally owned Oreo's sire. Earnest Wilson took Van Tyke to an APHA Championship as a young stallion.

It was both funny and scary before we left here tho.

I had saddled Oreo and since he was full of bull, turned him into my training pen to get some exercise while I finished getting ready to go. When I went back down there, he was standing in the corner, head turned looking at me, saddle hanging almost under his belly! What a guy! Didn't hurt the saddle at all. Most horses would have bucked and carried on until the saddle was demolished!

It was a struggle to get it unfastened because I had secured his halter rope to the horn and it was over his back with the weight of the saddle on it. Anyway, got it all off and re-saddled as my friend drove up so away we went with no delay.

I'll cinch tighter next time; he still has fat rounded withers. That will change in time.

Beautiful cool sunny day, shirtsleeve weather. Wonderful outing!

Good experience for Oreo. He hasn't been very many places. He was really, really FULL of himself but settled down and I got in a pretty good ride down there. The trainer seemed to like him.

## Spring, 1999

Oreo has continued to improve although my health has prevented me from riding him as much as I would like to. It's good that he is the kind that can have lengthy layoffs without it bringing out problems in him.

Again, people are wanting to breed to Oreo. I have made arrangements to have a very few mares artificially inseminated at Alpha Equine Hospital. Dr. Baker did a motility count and pronounced Oreo to have plenty of semen and high fertility.

The horse has a crooked penis which makes it hard for him to enter a mare. Using artificial insemination is a good route to go with him.

***Oreo and our mare Bar Moneys Pink***

My own mare, BAR MONEYS PINK is in foal to Oreo for February 2000. She was the first mare we tried inseminating, conceiving with one breeding.

This week in addition to Oreo getting another lesson in semen collection, I also spent an hour or so letting him learn how to be "staked out" on a rope. Using a soft long cotton rope tied to a tire in my training pen, I watched while Oreo figured out how not to get tangled up. This is not a horse that panics and the lesson went very well.

## May 8, 1999

As of this date, Oreo has three, babies on the way.

June 27, 1999

This has been a good week of experience for Oreo.

Miss Go Lasan has been in season all week and we have been live covering her every other day, including today (Sunday). Because of his physical limitations, it takes manually helping him. He has been pretty unruly up until now, probably out of frustration. However, with each cover he has improved - becoming a little easier to handle, and becoming more adept at what he is trying to do. Lasan has been a good mare to get this done with.

I have started using a rope halter, i.e., lariat rope fashioned into a halter that can exert considerable pressure, rather than O's regular halter. That has also helped to give me better control over his juvenile exuberance.

Today was the best day yet. I saddled him and left him tied under a shade tree for about 3 hours. Then about 3 p.m. I gave him a pretty fair workout. (Well as much workout as I could stand considering the heat and my age!) When I finished working him, I unsaddled him and put him back into his lot.

Then I got Lasan to check her with him. When teasing showed her to still be in heat, I put the breeding hobble and tail wrap on her and tied her under the shade tree.

When I went in to put the lariat on O, he dropped his head for it, was very very quiet, led perfectly out to the mare, although of course he got excited and attentive...he did NOT try to run over me, drag me or in any way misbehave . . . He sweet-talked Lasan and then moved into position and with my help did his deed. Being able to move into position to help guide his penis without someone else helping was a game-changer. I now can trust him during breeding.

Afterward he led quietly back to his lot. Perfect behavior. I couldn't ask him to be better than he was today. Now let us hope that Lasan will be in foal!

## August 1999

Miss Go Lasan will foal an Oreo baby in May of 2000, provided things go well and as scheduled! That gives me two of my own mares carrying his get, plus two belonging to other people. He got every mare in foal on his first try.

## September 1999

MY, it's been awhile since I tended to Oreo's Diary! So let me back up:

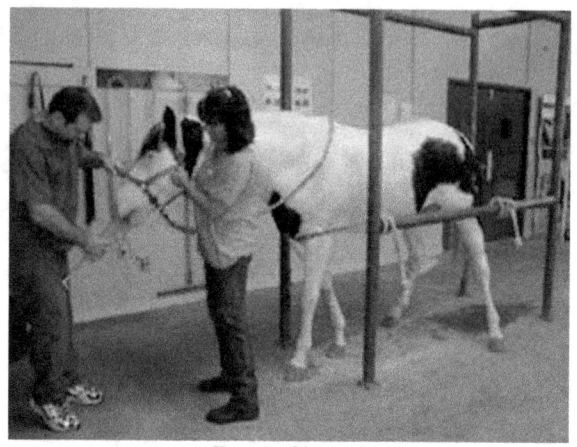

***Dental work***

Around the first of September, Oreo came up with an injured mouth. Evidently he was doing his mouthing thing on part of the fence, and hung his incisor, and when he had to pull hard to get loose, actually pulled two of his front teeth (upper) along with the gums, out of line with the others. I found him bleeding from the mouth that morning. The vet assures me that it will heal, the teeth are baby teeth which are about to shed sometime soon anyway, and that there should be no permanent disfigurement.

I thought I was going to have a permanently buck-toothed horse! It already looks a lot better.

# Wednesday, September 08, 1999

Yesterday we brought our four remaining cattle to the house and moved big round bales for them to feed on.

My plan is to work Oreo on them for a few weeks and then sell the calves and breed the cows.

I followed them around the middle trap on Oreo yesterday, letting them get used to him, and letting him watch them. This is the first day he has been around cattle since last year when I had the two yearlings here and played with them a couple of times. At that time, he "hooked on" almost immediately, and showed tremendous interest.

I didn't try to separate any of them yesterday, just followed them, turned them as a group, moved them from one end of the pen to the other, etc.

Today I used Oreo to move them from the middle trap into the south trap and the training pen. Once in the pen, we moved them from one end to the other, turned the group on the fence, separated one or two at a time and moved them opposite direction, etc.

Then I opened the gate into the barn/pen and moved them all into it, then separated one calf back out into the large pen.

Out there we could head the calf and move it out, and block it as it tried to go to its mother.

Oreo really wants to do something with these cattle. By the time the little session was over, he was pivoting and moving out with the calf to block it as best as he knew how at this point.

My feeling today is that if I were to let a professional cutting trainer ride him in among cattle, that trainer would really want me to put this horse in training. No question, Oreo has inherited the cutting instinct.

When we quit the cows, I took Oreo back into the middle trap and rode him awhile there, working on stop and turn, back uphill, etc. Then I dropped the bridle and rode him with just the halter and lead rope to see if I could. He really did well today. I'm very pleased and he is a joy to ride.

## October 16-17, 1999

OREO had his first overnighter in a coliseum this weekend. We went to Wichita Falls, TX to the Horse Expo, and exhibited him on "Stallion Row" with about 98 other stallions. I took the opportunity to ride him through all the big barns, up and down the streets, through the parking lots, and even down along the Wichita River, which splits the city-show grounds in two.

He could not have been better. Just a perfect gentleman. What a neat horse and what a great mind.

## November 1999

On a Saturday afternoon this month, after being hale and hearty in the a.m. and cleaning up all his regular breakfast, Oreo was obviously not well at 4 pm.

Since he had some mud on a shoulder, I thought possibly he had slipped and fallen while playing and maybe he was sore. So I turned him out in the back yard to graze and watched to see how he would move. He nibbled very little at the grass and then showed signs of discomfort.

Praying for my horse, I immediately called for a vet: I had to call three to catch one available via his beeper ... dear Dr. Gieb came within the hour and spent over 3 hours here with us, and finally recommended that I take Oreo to a specialty equine hospital near Dallas just in case the problem was going to require surgery. He remembered only too well, I'm sure, how devastated I was when my good buckskin Quarter Horse died some time back. He stressed that he thought Oreo was going to be fine, but "just in case" ...

I called my friend Erna who came to go with me; she'd been there before and could help me find the equine hospital. However, we got into all kinds of road construction and traffic, and got lost! We ended up at the famous Mustangs of Las Colinas sculptures, but at least that gave us a bearing on where we were, and we managed to get back on track and found the hospital shortly.

So at 10 pm I was in Las Colinas at the hospital and Oreo was getting a complete going over by the vets there. I left him with them after all his vital signs indicated he was not in any real danger. They wanted to monitor him for 24 hours, which they did and then I went over and brought him home.

He had to be eased onto his feed after all the stress, but other than that appeared to be doing fine ... UNTIL Monday afternoon when his temperature shot up to 104.5 degrees.

My usual vet who has offices within 2 miles of my house, was still in his office, so I rushed up there and consulted him, and came home with a fresh vial of penicillin and some paste Bute ... gave that to him and monitored his temp. Bill, the vet, had said that if the fever did not come down, to rush him back to Las Colinas. His fear was that there might be a problem in the gut, maybe even a hole.

But, thank the blessed Lord, within two hours of administering the Bute, Oreo's temperature was normal.

No further occurrences. Except that my Discover card is suffering severe stress from all these vet bills.

## December 22, 1999  Funny Oreo

It has been cold and windy for a few days plus I haven't been well, so Oreo has not been ridden. Today it was not windy and I was feeling somewhat better.

He's so funny! This afternoon when I went to feed him he literally begged me to play! Now remember, playing with a 1200 pound stallion can be hazardous to one's health! ... HOWEVER, sucker that I am, I stayed and played with him for awhile. I retrieved his ball from where he had thrown it over the fence, and bounced it off him a few times, untangled his lariat rope and tossed it over his head and back a few times ... letting him have the fun of grabbing it and snatching it off, naturally ... plus we played "Oreo chases the fat lady until she sticks the whip in his face and hollers 'BACK UP!' " ... then he backs up and pulls that con-artist bit of looking like "Who me? I just was playing, mama!" hahahahaha

**But please dear reader, don't try this at home.**

Now when a horse passes up his feed to play with a human being like a puppy (sort of), that is playful! Horses usually have one thing on their minds: FOOD (kind of like me ... I think I was a horse in a former life, or preparing to be one in the next) .

## February 2000

I took Oreo to an open show near Weatherford, TX and just rode him and worked him in the surrounding areas. Excellent experience for him. This was just his second time to go to an event with crowds, trailers and such, and although I decided not to enter anything (show was running v-e-r-y long and late) However, he was responsive and calm enough that I could have.

## February 17, 2000

THE BIG DAY. The first of Oreo's 4 year 2000 foals (the first of his foals, EVER) arrived this morning. Looks like a good filly, and she certainly seems to be the right color: buckskin.

*Baby Cookie meets her dad*

## February, A WEEK LATER OR SO ...

SPOTS AND DOTS RANCH gets a BLACK AND WHITE TOVERO FILLY from Oreo and Debby's good mare, Sky Bug. Marked a lot like Oreo and with excellent conformation and nice head!

*Van Tykes Skybug, Day One*

## March 25, 2000

BREEDING SEASON. Five outside mares at the present. Collection is being done at Cottar 2X4 Ranch as well as Alpha Equine. Getting "collected" is becoming routine for Oreo; now he is getting some new discipline as well. Going to be a genuine learning experience/spring for him!

### April 19

OREO has another daughter. This one is bay with wide blaze, but no other spots that are evident. Nice, heavy muscled, big strong filly. The owners are thrilled with her.

## May 19

LASAN foals ANOTHER Filly ... her 6th out of a total of 7 foals! This one, guess what, is most definitely a PAINT!

*The Foals of 2000, all Fillies*

## June 24 - end of breeding season 2000

NEXT SPRING will be fun, seeing the new crop of Oreo foals. We had a nice variety of mares to his court this year.

Sad News from Debbie Rogers at Spots n Dots: Her mare Trudy aborted twins from Oreo. The twins had gone undetected on a sonogram so it was a sad shock.

## Autumn 2000

I've talked to Earnest Wilson about fitting Oreo for the Stock Show in January. Having no enclosed stall to keep the horse in to keep him clean, I need him where that can be done. I explain to Earnest that I want him shown in trail and that I have him working all obstacles.

Oreo goes to Earnest late in December. I tell Earnest to enter Oreo at the stock show in trail and even though he will have a winter coat, I think he will be ok. I want to ride him in amateur trail there. Earnest reminds me that there isn't much time to get him ready. I reply that's OK, I don't expect to be a serious contender, just need a place to start where they can discipline him and get him used to crowds and behaving himself. And most of all keep him clean enough to show!

## January 16, 2001

OREO's three Fort Worth Stock Show classes: Amateur Stallions at halter; Novice Amateur Trail; Junior Trail.

I'm showing in the two amateur classes. I have told Earnest that I want them to show him in Junior Trail. Two trail patterns to memorize are just one too many for this old lady! Earnest has his son-in-law Shawn show Oreo in Junior Trail.

This is a four-judge show.

RESULTS:  Amateur Stallions -2nd under all 4 judges; Novice Amateur Trail  - 2nd, 3rd, 3rd, 4th under the four judges; Junior Trail -  1st, 2nd, 2nd, 3rd

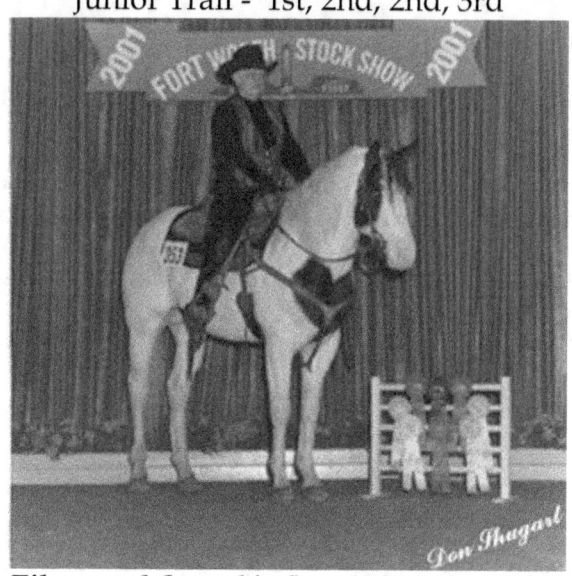

*Eileen and Oreo, his first APHA show 2001*
Sidebar:  Within the week tentative bookings for the 2001 season began coming in .....

# February 11 - Waco, Tx APHA Show.

Oreo places 2nd at halter, 5th in Junior Trail and in Novice Trail.

### February 16 - San Antonio Stock Show

Oreo places in trail again. No additional points are earned however.

## February 24, 2001

The first foals of the season arrived at the home of Paul and Jewell Walters, Georgetown, TX.

## April, 2001

Annie Calling Chief, owned by Thanh and Carol Ho of Colorado Springs, CO., has a chestnut tobiano filly from Oreo.

### July 2001

I am working Oreo, getting him ready to go back to Earnest Wilson for the fall Paint Show Season.

### August, 2001

OREO went back to Earnest Wilson and made four fall shows, including the Margarita in Fort Worth, and the Paint Performance Super Stakes in Glen Rose.

He returned home the first week in November with additional points in Junior Trail, plus a point in Heading, and money earned at the Super Stakes in Heading and Heeling.

Three Oreo foals competed in the 2001 PPHSS Futurity, our Oreo Pinkstuff Cookie and Lasan Van Tyke, and Debbie Rogers' filly Van Tykes Skybug. Debbie's filly won the futurity and our two placed nicely.

2001 PPHSS Futurity
Oreo Pinkstuff Cookie, Lasan Van Tyke, Van Tykes Skybug
***Three Fillies by Oreo competing at the
2001 PPHSS Futurity***

# December, 2001

I was impressed with the PAT PARELLI and LEON HARRELL demonstration during the 2001 NCHA Futurity in Fort Worth, and decided to invest in the first part of the program for Oreo's benefit.

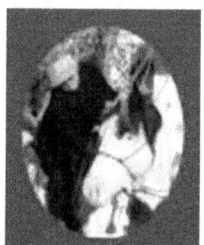

***Oreo and Me, winter 2001/2002***

After only a few days, OREO was relaxing more, enjoying me more, and I am certainly enjoying him to the fullest. I'm now riding him in the Parelli hackamore, which is basically a tied rope halter with a mecate'. What a nice boy my big O is.

# January, 2002

OREO in his first class as a senior at the 2002 Fort Worth Stock Show APHA Show. Not a bad showing for his first time with the big boys, garnering a 6th in Heading.

*That's me, keeping Oreo quiet and letting him watch*
*the other ropers coming out of the box.*
*Excitable, isn't he?*
*not good quality but a picture never the less :-)*

**Sidebar: APHA SHOW NOTES**

- 7 points in open Trail
- 1 point in amateur trail
- 1 point in heading
- 8 point in heeling
- 2 points in steer stopping

# March 21, 2002

ORO VAN TYKE, Overo COLT from Oreo and Bar Moneys Pink. Full brother to Oreo Pinkstuff Cookie. Our only foal this year.

*Salt Creek Open Show Grand Champion Stallion*
*ORO VAN TYKE - Age 4 months.*
*First time away from home - First show*
*- weaned TWO days previously*

## September 2002:

OREO is so quiet and good in his "Parelli" hackamore, that I rode and showed him in it (even though it is not "show legal" ... not severe enough apparently for a six year old horse! haha) at a rather large all-breed show, twice in April.

*Salt Creek Horse Show, riding Oreo in a halter*

I rode him in Western Pleasure for the second time at this show. He did quite nicely. I had entered him in another show last fall where I rode him with a snaffle and rope noseband. He was good there, too. But just look at what he is wearing in this photo. And look at his quiet willing stride. And NO, I will never ask him to roll peanuts. haha

# ASSORTED PHOTOS OF OREO'S GET

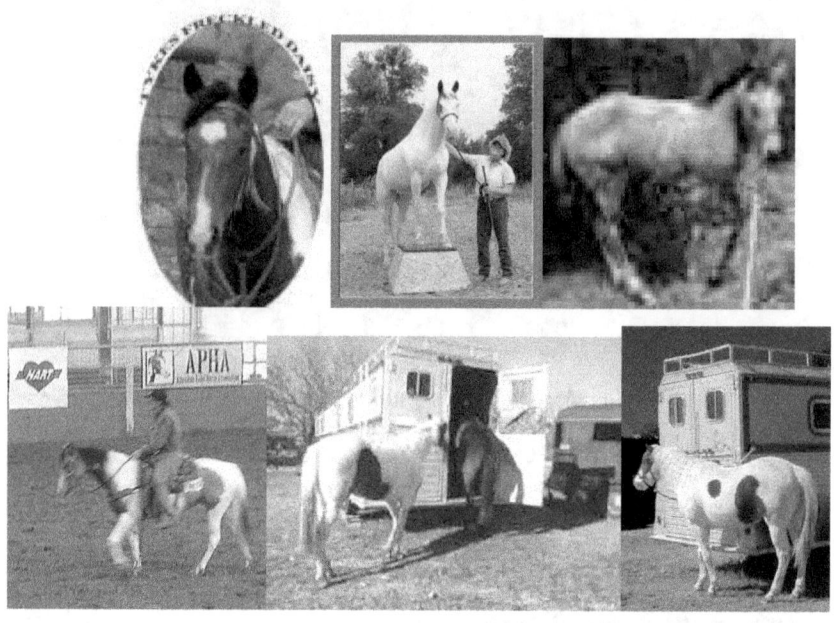

*A few of Oreo's offspring*

*PPHSS Futurity, Oreo and his get that were showing*

## OREO'S MAJOR SURGERY

The problems with gutteral pouch infections with Oreo had become so chronic that we consulted with Dr Jeff Folan of Weatherford Equine Hospital about surgery. Oreo was scheduled and with us watching from the observation room above the surgery suite, he was sedated and two surgeries done to correct his laryngeal problem. Although not a cure for the chronic gutteral pouch infections, the laryngeal surgery is to solve his roaring and shortness of breath.

Oreo spent over a week at the hospital and recovered well.

Harlan and I had won a trip to Puerto Villarta earlier in the summer, and once Oreo's surgery was done and his recovery complete, we scheduled our trip. We simply could not have gone while this was on our minds. We had a good time and when we got home Oreo and I were ready to resume our showing and fun times.

Extra pictures:

*2008 at a show with his son Silver and daughter Nellie*

## 2004 and 2005

*Showing at Paint Performance Super Stakes Shows*

## 2006 - Oreo is gelded at age 10

After considering it for three years, we became comfortable with the idea of Oreo becoming a gelding. No hormones raging, and even though he was a very well-behaved stallion, we feel that he will be a happier horse all the time now. And we will be welcome on trail rides and other activities, where sometimes participants are not comfortable around stallions. Oreo went into the hospital in early autumn to be gelded. He did well.

He was shown in the Paint Performance Super Stakes Finals a few weeks after being gelded. As always, he did well. We plan to show Oreo from time to time. I'm doing a little showing on his daughter Oreo Pinkstuff Cookie.

# OREO PINKSTUFF COOKIE

Cookie has been with Earnest Wilson for a few weeks this fall, and is headed for the Paint Performance Horse Super Stakes Finals. Cookie won her first APHA points in West Texas earlier this fall.

*Oreo Pinkstuff Cookie and Eileen at the inaugural American Paint Horse Association Ranch Horse Show.*

# 2007

Bar Moneys Pink bore Oreo's final foal May 2007, a buckskin filly that we named Nellie Finale', as the grand finale of Oreo's siring career.

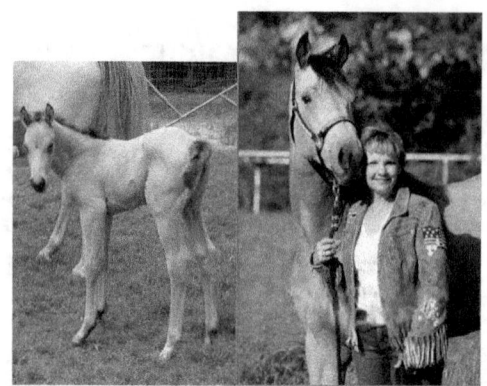

*Nellie Finale left; Nellie and Renita, Right*

Longe Line Champion
2008
Wichita Falls, TX

*Renita Massey, Amy Andresen and Nellie Finale*

*Nellie now belongs to Dianne Lindig*

# 2010

IN 2010 we gave Oreo to our wonderful friend, Renita Massey. Following is the story of Oreo under her partnership with him.

The much-beloved gelding Oreo Van Tyke, versatile show horse and a former prolific stallion, began a new career and developed a new community of admirers at age 14.

Under his new owner's guidance, he's helping children and adults with various mental and physical disabilities at a Therapeutic Riding Center 20 miles south of downtown Dallas.

Renita Massey of Midlothian had owned his final offspring, Nellie Finale. Renita and Eileen had been fast friends for a good while.

Renita was joyful at acquiring Oreo stating, "He has a lifetime home with me."

Riding him for her own pleasure and hoping to show him eventually, she said, "He settled right into my level - relaxed, but very responsive."

She also began taking him when needed as a therapy horse at the equine therapy center, where she is a volunteer and director.

*Oreo showing with a handicapped child at the APHA World Show*

"He is phenomenal with the kids," she says. "He's very intelligent and especially careful when a child is on his back. Some of our riders are non-verbal. Horses are the same way. So there's a kinship between them that is very moving to see. Oreo's name and personality have made him a real favorite at the barn."

At the 2010 APHA World Show's competition for special needs riders, Oreo was right at home in the limelight with Austin Eddy and Parker Johnson.

Eileen was in the stands. "It brought tears to my eyes," she said, "to see Oreo enabling these handicapped children to compete in the show. I think this is the crowning jewel of his career."

*Lining up for awards*

Bonding with the former stallion, Renita found him a wonderful partner on trail rides, cattle clinics, and in parades; She enjoyed him for almost two years.

*Renita and Oreo, Christmas Parade*

## A Short Life ...

**Often prone to colic, Oreo** got sick and died at a cattle working weekend in central Texas. Despite the efforts of a major equine hospital, he could not be saved.

**We'll always remember his hilarious personality; he had a good time all his life.**

**He will always be remembered.**

**This isn't the end of Oreo Van Tyke:** his foals live on in the true tradition of his life, competing, giving joy to their humans, and carrying on the bloodlines of this remarkable stallion. Here are a few of them ...

*Oreo Pinkstuff Cookie, Nellie Finale', Daisy*